My First Pocket Guide

SOUTH CAROLINA

By Carole Marsh

The GALLOPADE GANG

Carole Marsh	Kathy Zimmer	Cranston Davenport
Bob Longmeyer	Terry Briggs	Lisa Stanley
Chad Beard	Pat Newman	Antoinette Miller
Cecil Anderson	Billie Walburn	Victoria DeJoy
Steven Saint-Laurent	Jackie Clayton	Al Fortunatti
Jill Sanders	Pam Dufresne	Shery Kearney

Published by GALLOPADE INTERNATIONAL

www.southcarolinaexperience.com
800-536-2GET • www.gallopade.com

©2001 Carole Marsh • First Edition • All Rights Reserved.
Character Illustrations by Lucyna A. M. Green.
No part of this publication may be reproduced in whole or in part, stored in a retrieval system, or transmitted in any form or by any means, electronic, mechanical, photocopying, recording or otherwise, without written permission from the publisher.

The South Carolina Experience logo is a trademark of Carole Marsh and Gallopade International, Inc. A free catalog of The South Carolina Experience Products is available by calling 800-536-2GET, or by visiting our website at www.southcarolinaexperience.com

Gallopade is proud to be a member of these educational organizations and associations:

Other South Carolina Experience Products

- The South Carolina Experience!
- The BIG South Carolina Reproducible Activity Book
- The South Carolina Coloring Book
- My First Book About South Carolina!
- South Carolina "Jography": A Fun Run Through Our State
- South Carolina Jeopardy!: Answers and Questions About Our State
- The South Carolina Experience! Sticker Pack
- The South Carolina Experience! Poster/Map
- Discover South Carolina CD-ROM
- South Carolina "Geo" Bingo Game
- South Carolina "Histo" Bingo Game

A Word From the Author... (okay, a few words)...

Hi!
Here's your own handy pocket guide about the great state of South Carolina! It really will fit in a pocket—I tested it. And it really will be useful when you want to know a fact you forgot, to bone up for a test, or when your teacher says, "I wonder . . ." and you have the answer—instantly! Wow, I'm impressed!

Get smart, have fun!
Carole Marsh

South Carolina Basics

South Carolina Geography

South Carolina History

South Carolina People

South Carolina Places

South Carolina Nature

South Carolina Miscellany

South Carolina Basics explores your state's symbols and their special meanings!

South Carolina Geography digs up the what's where in your state!

South Carolina History is like traveling through time to some of your state's great moments!

South Carolina People introduces you to famous personalities and your next-door neighbors!

South Carolina Places shows you where you might enjoy your next family vacation!

South Carolina Nature - no preservatives here, just what Mother Nature gave to South Carolina!

All the real fun stuff that we just HAD to save for its own section!

3

State Name

Who Named You?

South Carolina's official state name is...

South Carolina

State Name

Word Definition

OFFICIAL: appointed, authorized, or approved by a government or organization

Statehood: May 23, 1788

South Carolina was the eighth state to ratify the United States Constitution and join the Union.

South Carolina was the eighth state honored on a commemorative quarter, starting in May 2000. Look for it in cash registers everywhere!

Coccinella noemnotata is my name (that's Latin for ladybug)! What's YOURS?

4

State Name Origin

A Name of Royal Proportions!

State Name Origin

England's King Charles I named the region south of Virginia *Carolana*, meaning "Land of Charles." This is derived from the Latin name *Carolus*, translated as "Charles." In 1663, Charles II changed the spelling to Carolina. The territory was later divided between North and South Carolina.

North and South Carolina were one colony until 1712.

State Nickname

WHO Are You Calling Names?

State Nickname

Palmetto State

South Carolina is not the only name by which our state is recognized. Like many other states, South Carolina has a nickname, official or unofficial!

How did South Carolina get its nickname?

In 1776, during the Revolutionary War, England attacked Fort Moultrie which was built on Sullivan's Island to protect the city of Charles Town. The fort was made of palmetto logs. The wooden logs were made from the region's plentiful palmetto trees. English ships attacked Fort Moultrie, but their cannonballs just sank into the soft wooden walls of the fort. The Americans won the Battle of Fort Moultrie and South Carolina became known as the "Palmetto State."

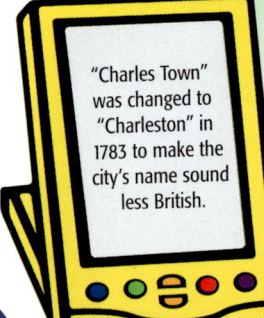

"Charles Town" was changed to "Charleston" in 1783 to make the city's name sound less British.

State Capital/Capitol

State Capital:
Columbia
Founded in 1786

State Capital/Capitol

Capital Since 1790

South Carolina leaders chose Columbia as the state's capital (replacing Charles Town) because it was near the state's geographical center. Columbia grew from fields and woods to a planned city with wide, straight streets. Today, Columbia is the state's largest city.

The South Carolina State House (capitol) is in Columbia. There are six bronze stars on the State House walls. The stars mark spots where Union cannonballs hit the building during the Civil War.

Word Definition

CAPITAL: a town or city that is the official seat of government
CAPITOL: the building in which the government officials meet

State Government

Who's in Charge Here?

South Carolina's GOVERNMENT has three branches:

- LEGISLATIVE
- EXECUTIVE
- JUDICIAL

State Government

LEGISLATIVE: The legislative branch is called the General Assembly. Two Houses: Senate (46 members) House of Representatives (124 members)

EXECUTIVE: A governor, lieutenant governor, state treasurer, secretary of state, and department heads

JUDICIAL: Supreme Court (5 members) Court of Appeals Circuit Courts Lower courts include Probate Courts, Magistrates' Courts, Recorders' Courts and Family Courts

When you are 18 and register according to South Carolina laws, you can vote! So please do! Your vote counts!

South Carolina's current constitution was adopted in 1895. It has been amended, or changed, hundreds of times.

8

State Flag

State Flag

South Carolina's current state flag was adopted in 1861. It was designed in 1775 by Colonel William Moultrie for South Carolina troops to carry during the Revolutionary War. Moultrie made the flag blue to match the color of the uniforms the soldiers wore. He put a silver crescent (shaped like a quarter moon) on the flag because most men had this emblem on their caps. Later he placed a silver palmetto tree in the flag's center to represent to the palmetto-log fort on Sullivan's Island where Moultrie defeated the British.

As you travel throughout South Carolina, count the times you see the South Carolina flag! Look for it on government vehicles, too!

State Seal & Motto

State Seal

The state seal of South Carolina features two ovals side by side. The left side shows a picture of a palmetto tree. The right side shows a figure of Hope holding a laurel branch. These represent the desire of the state to be free and independent forever.

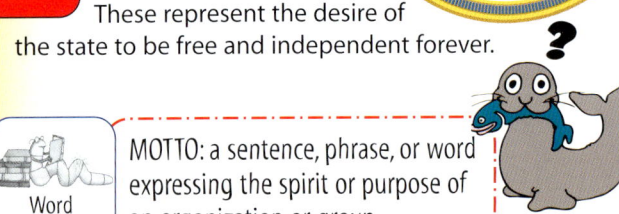

Word Definition
MOTTO: a sentence, phrase, or word expressing the spirit or purpose of an organization or group

State Motto

South Carolina has two state mottoes:

South Carolina's state seal was adopted in 1776.

Animis Opibusque Parati
(Prepared in Mind and Resources)

Dum Spiro Spero
(While I Breathe, I Hope)

10

State Birds

Birds of a Feather

Carolina Wren
South Carolina's state bird, the Carolina wren, likes to build its nest on farm buildings. Its song helps South Carolinians wake up and start the day!

Wild Turkey
South Carolina's state game bird, the wild turkey, can weigh as much as 20 pounds (9 kilograms) and provided many a feast for early South Carolina pioneer families.

State Birds

State Tree

PALMETTO

"Woodman, spare that tree!" —George Pope Morris

State Tree

Palmetto trees grow abundantly in South Carolina. They are also known as sabal palmettos and cabbage palmettos. These trees have clusters of large fan-shaped leaves topping a thick stalk or trunk about 20–80 feet (6–24 meters) high. Palmettos have long been a part of South Carolina history.

State Flower

Yellow Jasmine

A lovelier flower on earth was never sown. —William Wordsworth

State Flower

South Carolina's state flower is pretty to look at and pleasant to smell! Carolina jasmine is a climbing vine with evergreen foliage and bright yellow flowers. It's actually a member of the olive family!

The Yellow Jasmine is also known as the Carolina Jessamine!

RIDDLE:
If the state flower got mixed up with the state bird, what would you have?

ANSWER: A fragrant yellow turkey!

State Animal

White-tailed Deer

State Animal

The white-tailed deer is the most common variety of deer in South Carolina. It is found throughout the state, especially in South Carolina's pine forests.

The Boykin Spaniel is South Carolina's state dog. It was first bred by South Carolina hunters to provide an ideal dog for hunting ducks and wild turkeys.

State Reptile

LOGGERHEAD TURTLE

State Reptile

Loggerhead turtles live off South Carolina's coast. These turtles crawl ashore to lay their eggs in the sand. Each female turtle digs a hole in the sand, lays up to 150 golf-ball-sized eggs in this nest, and then returns to the ocean. When baby turtles hatch, they crawl out of the sand and head to the water. It's a race for survival as they try to make it to the ocean before they are caught by raccoons, seagulls, or dogs.

The spotted salamander is South Carolina's state amphibian.

People are working to protect turtles by roping off beach areas where turtles lay eggs. Restrictions have also been placed on nighttime lights near nesting areas so the turtles will come ashore.

State Dances

Shag

South Carolina's state dance is called the shag. You dance the shag to beach music, a distinct type of rhythm and blues. It began in the late 1930s–40s at The Pad, a popular dance club in Ocean Drive, "OD" in North Myrtle Beach. "Doin' the shag" is a beach tradition that continues today.

State Dances

Square Dance

South Carolina also has a state folk dance. It's the square dance. Square dancing is popular in upcountry South Carolina, especially at Hillbilly Day in the town of Mountain Rest.

South Carolina has two State Songs. They are *Carolina*, and *South Carolina on My Mind*. Do you know them?

State Fruit and Beverages

State Fruit: Peach

South Carolina leads all other states in the production of peaches!

State Beverage: Milk

More than 33,000 milk cows help South Carolina dairy farmers provide this delicious and nutritious drink!

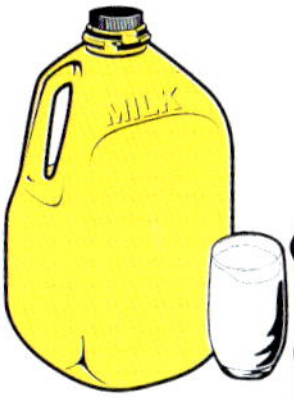

Moooo!

South Carolina Milkshake

Mix 2 scoops of vanilla ice cream, 1 cup of milk, and slices of 1 South Carolina peach in a blender. Yummy!

State Hospitality Beverage: Tea

South Carolina was the first state to grow tea and the only state to produce it for business when it adopted tea as its official hospitality beverage on April 30, 1995. The Charleston Tea Plantation on Wadmalaw Island is open to visitors who wish to see tea grown and harvested.

17

State Stone, Gemstone, and Shell

State Stone:
Blue Granite

South Carolina is one of the top 10 producers of granite among the 50 states. Granite is an igneous rock. It is commonly used as a building stone.

State Stone, Gemstone, and Shell

State Gemstone:
Amethyst

The amethyst is a variety of quartz that is bluish-violet in color.

State Shell:
Lettered Olive

Olive shells are shiny and often feature v-shaped patterns. They are most often brown and white. Native Americans wore olive shells as jewelry.

State Bugs

State Insect:
Carolina Mantid

A mantid is a praying mantis; beneficial in controlling harmful insects, and easily recognizable throughout the state.

State Butterfly:
Eastern Tiger Swallowtail

Swallowtails have black wings with yellow stripes. Sometimes the females are all-black. These insects like to eat sugary flower nectar.

State Fish

Striped Bass

This fish is popular with South Carolina fishermen. They are common in many lakes. State parks sponsor fishing tournaments for children and families. You can enter—maybe you'll catch *THE BIG ONE*!

State Fish

South Carolina Striped Bass

Put a bass filet on foil. Drizzle with lemon juice. Sprinkle with salt and pepper. Add shredded smoked ham and broil fish until done.

Sounds fishy to me!

20

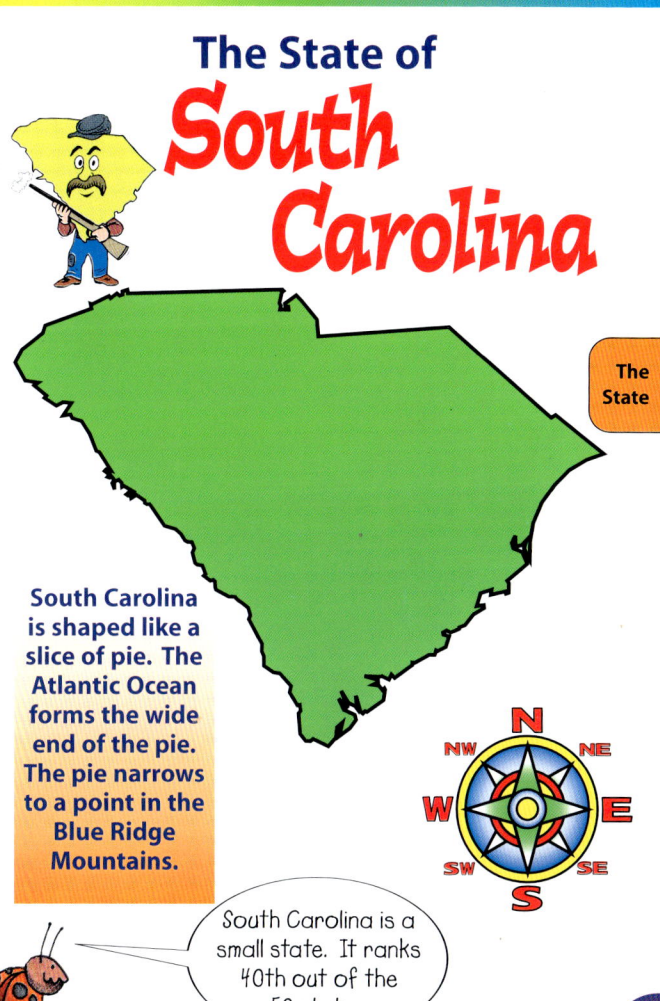

State Location

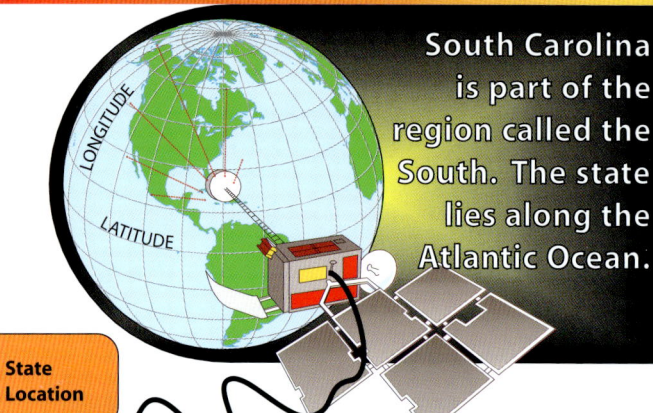

South Carolina is part of the region called the South. The state lies along the Atlantic Ocean.

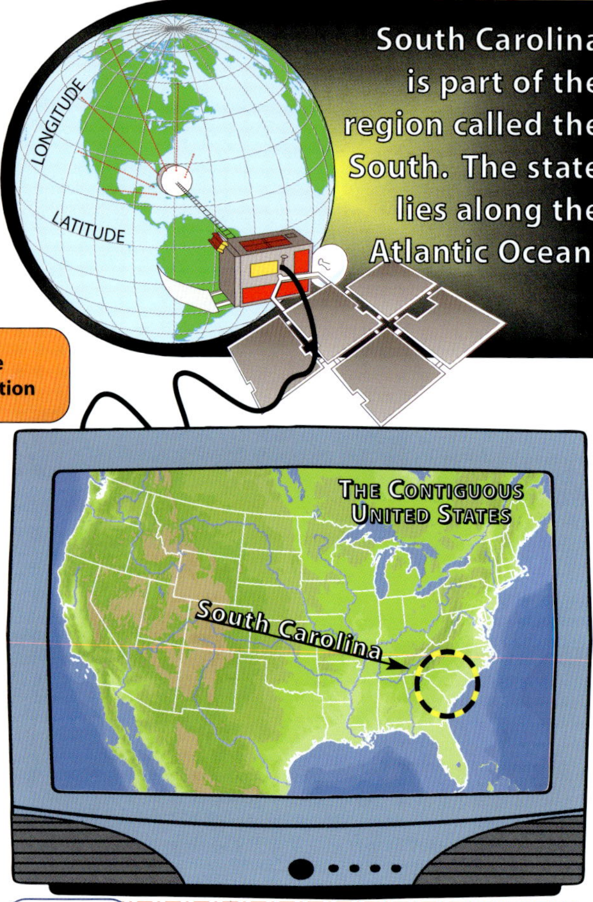

State Location

Word Definition

LATITUDE: Imaginary lines which run horizontally east and west around the globe
LONGITUDE: Imaginary lines which run vertically north and south around the globe

State Neighbors

These border South Carolina:

States: North Carolina, Georgia

Body of water: Atlantic Ocean

A rock in the Sumter National Forest marks the point where the borders of South Carolina, North Carolina, and Georgia meet. The rock is called Ellicott's Rock, named for surveyor Andrew Ellicott.

State Neighbors

East-West, North-South, Area

I'll Take the Low Road...

East-West, North-South, Area

South Carolina stretches 218 miles (351 kilometers) from north to south—or south to north. Either way, it's a long drive!

Total Area: Approximately 31,189 square miles (80,780 square kilometers)
Land Area: Approximately 30,111 square miles (77,987 square kilometers)

South Carolina is 275 miles (443 kilometers) from east to west—or west to east. Either way, it's *still* a long drive!

Highest & Lowest Points

You Take the High Road!

Highest & Lowest Points

HIGHEST POINT
SASSAFRAS MOUNTAIN—3,560 FEET (1,085 METERS)

The Blue Ridge Mountains cover about 500 square miles (1,295 square kilometers) in the northwest corner of the state. Sassafras Mountain rises in the Blue Ridge, part of the Appalachian Mountain chain.

LOWEST POINT
SEA LEVEL ALONG THE ATLANTIC COAST

25

State Counties

I'm County-ing on You!

South Carolina is divided into 46 counties.

State Counties

Word Definition — COUNTY: an administrative subdivision of a state or territory

South Carolina's capital, Columbia, is in Richland County.

1, 2, 3, 4, 5...

6, 7, 8, 9, 10...

26

Natural Resources

It's All Natural!

Two-thirds of South Carolina is forest. South Carolina's state tree, the palmetto, grows along the coast. Cypress, oak, magnolia, and tulip trees grow in the swamps and lowlands. Pine, maple, hemlock, and beech trees grow inland.

Natural Resources

Word Definition

NATURAL RESOURCES: things that exist in or are formed by nature

Minerals and rocks:
Granite
Limestone

Commercial fishing in South Carolina is restricted to saltwater fish and shellfish caught in the ocean. Crabs, shrimp, oysters, and clams are some of the most common catch.

South Carolina also produces clay, barite, cyanite, vermiculite, and mica.

27

Weather

Weather, Or Not?!

South Carolina's average temperatures can drop to 45°F (7°C) in the winter and reach 80°F (27°C) in the summer.

Weather

Highest temperature: 111°F (44°C), Camden, June 28, 1954

°F=Degrees Fahrenheit °C=Degrees Celsius

Lowest temperature: -20°F (-29°C), Caesar's Head, January 18, 1977

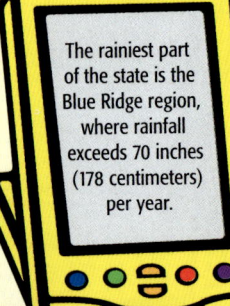

The rainiest part of the state is the Blue Ridge region, where rainfall exceeds 70 inches (178 centimeters) per year.

28

Topography

Back On Top

South Carolina's topography includes three distinct regions. The **Atlantic Coastal Plain** makes up the southeastern two-thirds of the state. This area is also called lowcountry. The **Piedmont Plateau** makes up most of the rest of the state. It's also known as upcountry. The northwestern tip of South Carolina rises into the third region: the **Blue Ridge Mountains**.

Sea Level
100 m / 328 ft
200 m / 656 ft
500 m / 1,640 ft
1,000 m / 3,281 ft
2,000 m / 6,562 ft
5,000 m / 16,404 ft

Topography

Word Definition
TOPOGRAPHY: the detailed mapping of the features of a small area or district

The **fall line** is the boundary between South Carolina lowcountry and upcountry.

Mountains and Ranges

King of the Hill
Mountains

The Blue Ridge Mountains cross into South Carolina at the northwestern tip of the state. The state's highest point, Sassafras Mountain, is part of this mountain range. The Cherokee Nation once inhabited the rugged Blue Ridge Mountains. Today, this scenic area is protected in the Andrew Pickens Division of Sumter National Forest.

Mountains and Ranges

Rivers & Lakes

A River Runs Through It!

These are some of South Carolina's major rivers:

- **Santee**—the state's longest at 143 miles (230 km)
- **Pee Dee**—the state's largest river
- **Broad**
- **Saluda**
- **Catawba**
- **Savannah**—along the South Carolina/Georgia border
- **Coosawhatchie**
- **Tyger**
- **Black**
- **Edisto**
- **Salkehatchie**
- **Congaree**
- **Santee**
- **Cooper**

Rivers & Lakes

The biggest lakes in the state are man-made.

- **Lake Marion**
- **Lake Moultrie**
- **Lake Greenwood**
- **Lake Wylie**
- **Lake Murray**
- **Hartwell Lake**
- **Lake Keowee**
- **Lake Wateree**

Grab a paddle!

South Carolina's Coast

South Carolina's coastal area includes beaches, islands, and saltwater marshes. The coastal area includes 13 major islands:

- Johns Island
- Seabrook Island
- Daufuskie Island
- Edisto Island
- Fripp Island
- Hilton Head – largest
- Hunting Island
- James Island
- Kiawah Island
- Parris Island
- St. Helena Island
- Sullivans Island
- Folly Island

South Carolina's Coast

The Grand Strand is the name of the area along South Carolina's northernmost coastline. Myrtle Beach is the largest of the many towns along this 60-mile (96-kilometer) stretch that are popular vacation destinations.

South Carolina has about 187 miles (301 kilometers) of coast when measured "as the crow flies" (in a straight line), but its many islands and bays give South Carolina 2,876 miles (4,628 kilometers) of coastline. South Carolina has more than 300 miles (483 kilometers) of sandy beaches.

Cities & Towns

ARE YOU A CITY MOUSE... OR A COUNTRY MOUSE?

Have you heard of these wonderful South Carolina town, city, or crossroad names? Perhaps you can start your own list!

Cities & Towns

MAJOR CITIES:
- Columbia
- Charleston
- North Charleston
- Greenville
- Spartanburg
- Sumter
- Rock Hill
- Hilton Head Island

UNIQUE NAMES:
- Ashepoo
- Fingerville
- Nine Times
- Ninety Six
- Pumpkintown
- Ruby
- Honea Path
- Thicketty

33

Transportation

Major Interstate Highways

I–20 I–385
I–26 I–77
I–95

Transportation

Railroads

South Carolina has over 2,500 miles (4,023 kilometers) of railroad track.

Major Airports

South Carolina has major airports in Columbia, Charleston, and the Greenville-Spartanburg area.

Seaports

Charleston Harbor, Georgetown Harbor, and Port Royal Harbor are three of South Carolina's major harbors. Oceangoing ships from all over the world dock here.

Timeline

1521	Spaniards from Santo Domingo visit South Carolina
1663	King Charles II issues charter to establish Carolina colony
1670	English establish first permanent settlement on the west bank of the Ashley River
1708	European population reaches 19,000
1776	South Carolina sends four delegates to Philadelphia to sign the Declaration of Independence
1780	British troops occupy Charles Town during the American Revolution
1786	Capital moves from Charles Town to Columbia
1788	South Carolina ratifies the U.S. Constitution, becomes eighth state to join the Union
1860	South Carolina secedes from the Union
1861	Civil War begins with Confederate attack on Union-held Fort Sumter
1865	Union army invades South Carolina and Confederate forces surrender at Appomattox
1867	Reconstruction begins; state re-establishes its government
1877	Planters and merchants establish Bourbon rule
1880	Textile industry is started
1923	Manufactured goods exceed agricultural goods for first time in state history
1975	James Edwards becomes first Republican governor in 100 years
2000	*H.L. Hunley* is raised off the South Carolina coast
2000	Confederate flag is retired from flying over the capitol in Columbia
2001	On to the 21st century

Timeline

Early History

Here come the humans!

Early History

Thousands of years ago, ancient peoples inhabited South Carolina. They may have originally come across a frozen bridge of land between Asia and Alaska. If so, they slowly traveled east until some settled in what would one day become the state of South Carolina. The early Indian settlers hunted and fished; those along the coasts dug for clams and oysters.

Around 2000 BC these settlers planted corn and squash. An estimated 15,000 natives belonging to 30 different tribes lived in South Carolina.

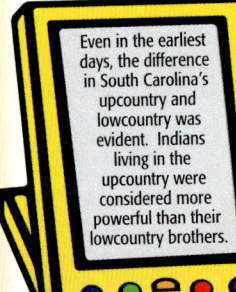

Even in the earliest days, the difference in South Carolina's upcountry and lowcountry was evident. Indians living in the upcountry were considered more powerful than their lowcountry brothers.

Early Indians

Native Americans Once Ruled!

The **Cherokee** lived in about 50 villages spread across the upcountry. They built dome-shaped houses out of sticks and bark. Each village contained a log council house. The Cherokee were excellent hunters. The **Catawba** also occupied the upcountry.

The **Yemassee** lived along the Carolina coast. Their habitats were smaller in size and more scattered than the Cherokee. Using dugout canoes to reach the oyster beds at low tide, they harvested oysters and clams and traded with neighboring tribes. The **Westo** tribe was feared by all. They were a small but mobile group some folks believed were cannibals!

Early Indians

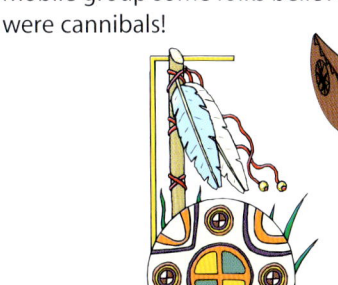

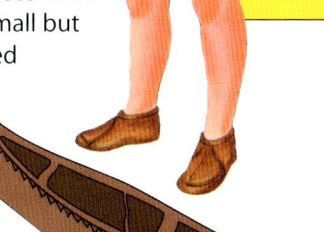

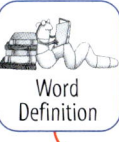

Word Definition

WAMPUM: beads, pierced and strung, used by Indians as money or for ornaments

37

Exploration

Land Ho!

The first explorers to visit present-day South Carolina were from Spain. In 1526, Vásquez de Ayllón settled near Georgetown, but his time in the lowcountry was brief. Disease and Indian attacks drove him and his settlers away.

Exploration

The French attempted a settlement near Port Royal in 1562 but they were equally unsuccessful.

It wasn't until 1670 when the English sailed up the Ashley River and settled Charles Town, that the area began to attract other Europeans.

Explorers, missionaries, and adventurers came from Europe on ships in the 1500s.

Colonization

Home, Sweet Home

The Carolina colony started in 1670 and grew from its early roots at Charles Town to an established settlement of more than 8,000 inhabitants by 1708. The majority of these people were slaves of African descent. The white settlers were English or French Huguenots who came to Carolina seeking religious freedom. The early colonists farmed and traded with the Indians. The first crop they grew was indigo which produced a blue dye sought after in Europe. They later learned to grow rice, a crop familiar to the African slaves. But life was not easy for the settlers. Disease and battles with Indians and rival Europeans made life difficult. Pirates often attacked ships along the coast, finding it easy to hide among the many small offshore islands. Blackbeard and Anne Bonney were among the most well-known pirates.

Colonization

Hardships didn't hamper growth and by 1721, the Carolina Colony was inhabited by 20,000 people!

Key Crops

Indigo and **rice** were the two major crops grown in the Carolina Colony's earliest days. **Wheat** and **tobacco** were also grown for export to other colonies and abroad from the port city of Charleston. After the Civil War, **cotton** replaced rice as the major crop. Cotton was a nonperishable product that was easy to sell.

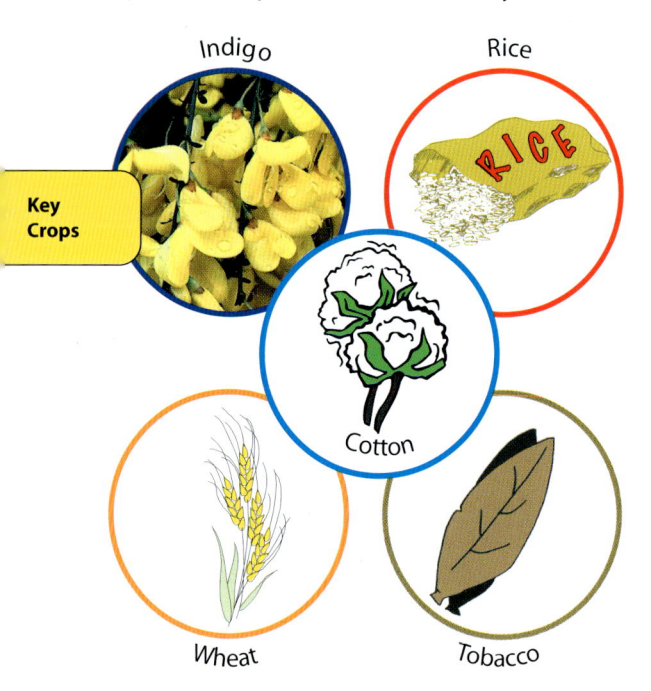

Indigo

Rice

Key Crops

Cotton

Wheat

Tobacco

40

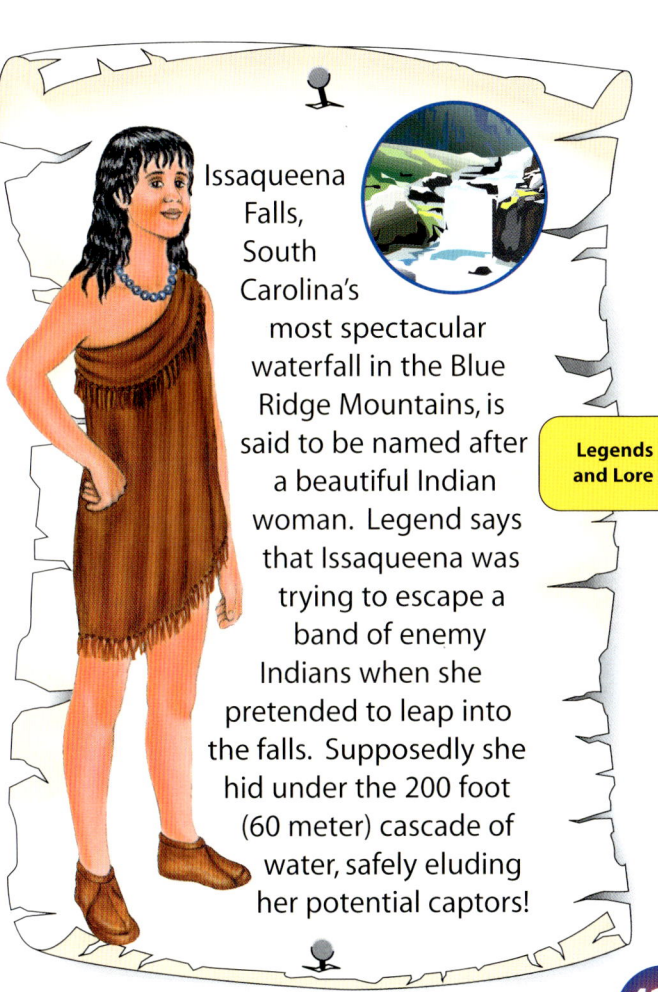

Legends and Lore

Issaqueena Falls, South Carolina's most spectacular waterfall in the Blue Ridge Mountains, is said to be named after a beautiful Indian woman. Legend says that Issaqueena was trying to escape a band of enemy Indians when she pretended to leap into the falls. Supposedly she hid under the 200 foot (60 meter) cascade of water, safely eluding her potential captors!

Legends and Lore

41

Revolution

Freedom! Freedom!

Some settlers in the New World felt that England ignored their ideas and concerns. In 1775, the colonies went to war with England. On July 4, 1776, the Declaration of Independence was signed. At least 140 Revolutionary War Battles took place on South Carolina soil. One of the most important was the Battle of Cowpens in 1781, where South Carolina soldiers took on an elite British unit, defeating them soundly. But South Carolina's people were split in allegiance to Great Britain. Many upcountry settlers continued to support the British during the revolution leading to internal battles between them and those fighting for independence.

Revolution

> The upcountry pioneers were mainly from Scotland and Ireland. They farmed in areas considered to be some of the wildest and most dangerous in the New World.

Slaves and Slavery

The life of a plantation slave was very difficult. Field hands worked as long as 15 hours a day. Their homes were often small, crowded, huts or shacks. Slaves were given small amounts of food by their owners such as meat, flour, milk, lard, cornmeal, and greens. They added wild fruits and nuts found in their environment to their diets.

Slaves and Slavery

Families were often separated and sold to different owners when members were placed on the auction block. Charleston's old slave market still stands; a grim reminder of South Carolina's plantation days.

Word Definition

ABOLITIONIST: person who believed slavery was wrong and should be ended

The Civil War

Brother

The Civil War was fought between the American states. The argument was over states' rights to make their own decisions, including whether or not to own slaves. Some of the southern states began to secede (leave) the Union. They formed the Confederate States of America. South Carolina was the first state to secede and the site of the first shot fired in the Civil War. This occurred at Fort Sumter, a federal fort located in Charleston Harbor. In the four war years to follow, about 63,000 soldiers fought in the Confederate Army, with one in four losing their life. South Carolina's citizens also suffered during the war, deprived of adequate supplies of medicine and food due to blockaded ports. Union General William Tecumseh Sherman cut a swath of destruction from Augusta, Georgia, to Columbia, South Carolina, where soldiers burned most of the city.

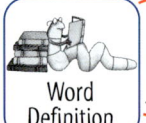

The Civil War

Word Definition

RECONSTRUCTION: the recovery and rebuilding period following the Civil War

The Civil War

vs. Brother

Soldiers often found themselves fighting against former friends and neighbors, even brother against brother. Those who did survive often went home without an arm, leg, or both, since amputation was the "cure" for most battlefield wounds. More Americans were killed during the Civil War than during World Wars I and II together!

The Civil War

In 1863, the Emancipation Proclamation, given by U.S. President Abraham Lincoln, freed the slaves still under Confederate control. Some slaves became sharecroppers; others went to Northern states to work in factories.

Famous Documents

Get It In Writing!

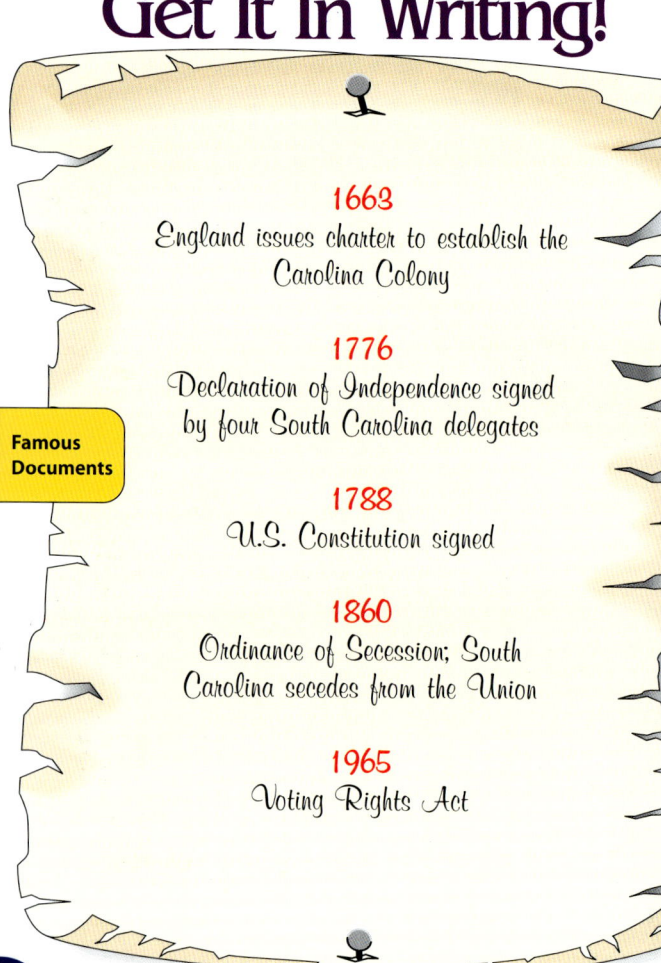

1663
England issues charter to establish the Carolina Colony

1776
Declaration of Independence signed by four South Carolina delegates

1788
U.S. Constitution signed

1860
Ordinance of Secession; South Carolina secedes from the Union

1965
Voting Rights Act

Famous Documents

Immigrants

WELCOME TO AMERICA!

People have come to South Carolina from other states and many other countries on almost every continent! As time goes by, South Carolina's population grows more diverse. This means that people of different races and from different cultures and ethnic backgrounds have moved to South Carolina.

Immigrants

In the past, many immigrants have come to South Carolina from Scotland and Ireland. More recently, people have migrated to South Carolina from Hispanic countries such as Mexico. The Greenville-Spartanburg area is home to many corporations with employees from countries such as France, Germany, the Netherlands and many others. Only a certain number of immigrants are allowed to move to America each year. Many of these immigrants eventually become U.S. citizens.

Disasters & Catastrophes!

1866

Earthquake rocks Charleston; thousands injured, sections of the city demolished; tremors felt 600 miles away!

1880

Baleen whale swims into Charleston Harbor; the whale is captured and its 40-foot (12-meter) skeleton is displayed at the Charleston Museum

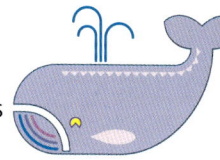

1885

Cyclone strikes Charleston

Disasters & Catastrophes!

1893

Hurricane ravages South Carolina coast; ranks as one of the highest weather fatality storms in history with 1,000–2,000 killed in South Carolina and neighboring Georgia

1968

Orangeburg Massacre takes lives of three black college students and leaves 27 wounded after clash with police over segregation of bowling alley

1989

Hurricane Hugo sweeps through South Carolina, taking 18 lives and leaving $5 billion in damage

Legal Stuff

1663
England's King Charles II issues charter for colonization of "Carolina"

1712
Colony divides into northern and southern regions

1860
South Carolina secedes from the Union

Legal Stuff

1895
State constitution rewritten to exclude blacks from voting

2000
Confederate flag removed from state capitol

Women & Children

Rebecca Brewton Motte—patriot of the Revolution; engineered the surrender of the British at "Fort Motte," with compliance and courtesy to the enemy

Elizabeth Allston Pringle—rice planter and writer who recorded her experiences during Reconstruction

Septima Poinsette Clark—teacher and civil rights activist who succeeded in having the Charleston County School District hire black teachers around 1920

Hannah English Williams—South Carolina's first woman biologist

Anne Pamela Cunningham—directed the restoration of George Washington's Virginia home, Mount Vernon

Wars

Fight! Fight! Fight!

Wars that had an impact on South Carolina include:
- **French and Indian Wars**
- **Revolutionary War**
- **War of 1812**
- **Mexican-American War**
- **Civil War**
- **Spanish-American War**
- **World War I**
- **World War II**
- **Korean War**
- **Vietnam War**
- **Persian Gulf War**

Wars

Claim to Fame

Living History

Charleston

Claim to Fame

South Carolina's history and its 187–mile (301 kilometer) coastline are its two claims to fame. Some of South Carolina's state parks include historical sites. The grave of American Revolutionary leader Thomas Sumter is located in Stateburg. Ruins of a 1696 colonial settlement can be found in Old Dorchester near Summerville. Andrew Jackson Historical State Park in Lancaster is in vicinity of his birthplace. Visiting Charleston makes history come to life with its pastel-painted homes, horse drawn carriages and Civil War cannons. Look for the basket ladies at the market. Weaving baskets from sweetgrass is a craft which has been passed along from mother to daughter for generations. Visitors to South Carolina's beaches can find sand dollars, crabs, and large cockle shells which were sometimes used to make pretty shapes on their pottery.

Indian Tribes

Mississippian   Yamasee
Cherokee   PeeDee
Catawba   Kiawah

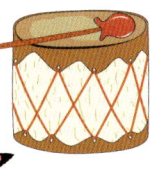

The largest Native American nation remaining in the state is the PeeDee. They can be found living in four northeast counties. The PeeDee have a representative council and two chiefs, one elected and one hereditary.

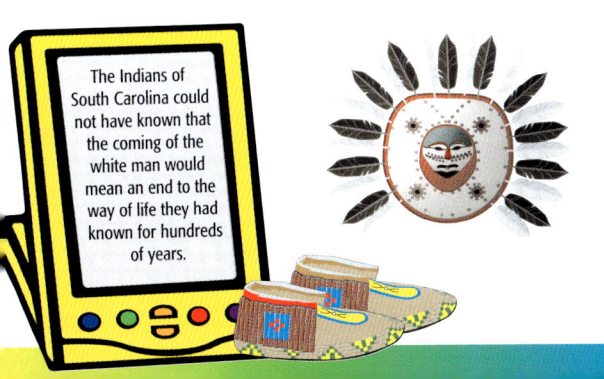

Indian Tribes

The Indians of South Carolina could not have known that the coming of the white man would mean an end to the way of life they had known for hundreds of years.

Explorers and Settlers

Here, There, Everywhere!

Lucas Vásquez de Ayllón—Established San Miguel de Gualdape in 1526, the first European colony in South Carolina

Jean Ribault—French Huguenot; established small colony in 1526 in Port Royal

William Sayle—helped to settle Charles Town in 1670 at Albemarle Point, about 10 miles (16 kilometers) up the Ashley River

Explorers and Settlers

Dr. Henry Woodward—lived with the Indians before the colonists' arrival; helped establish trade relations with the settlers and Indians; introduced rice cultivation

Robert Johnson—became South Carolina's colonial governor in 1730

Bon Voyage!

54

State Founders

Founding Fathers

Charles Pinckney—believed to have drafted an early plan for the U.S. Constitution

James Gadsden—railroad executive and diplomat in the 18th and 19th century; arranged for the Gadsden Purchase allowing U.S. to buy present-day New Mexico and Arizona from Mexico

Vandry McBee—planter; called the "Father of Greenville"

Founding Mothers

Judith Giton Manigault—French Huguenot and one of the first women settlers in Charles Town in 1685

Afra Harleston Coming—sailed to Charles Town around 1670; earned 100 acres (40 hectares) after two years servitude; married and managed plantation for seafaring husband

Henrietta Deering Johnston—pastel artist in the late 1600s and early 1700s; supported family after death of husband by painting portraits of famous people of the day

State Founders

55

Famous African-Americans

Mary McLeod Bethune—educator; worked to improve educational opportunities for blacks

Jesse Jackson—Baptist minister, civil-rights leader, and politician from Greenville

Denmark Vesey—former slave who engineered failed slave revolt in South Carolina

Famous African-Americans

Septima Poinsette Clark—educator and civil rights crusader

Modjeska Montieth Simkins—civil-rights pioneer

Augusta Baker—storyteller

Charlayne Hunter-Gault—journalist

Ghosts

DID SOMEONE SAY BOO!?

The clatter of hooves and the rumbling of a racing carriage can still be heard and seen on Hilton Head Island in the midst of a bone-chilling thunderstorm. Natives recognize the black carriage drawn by four black horses as Martin Bayard's carriage. Bayard was a handsome son of a well-to-do planter engaged to be married to the beautiful Victoria Stoney, daughter of one of the island's finest families. As fate would have it, Victoria was struck with a fatal fever and died on the eve of her wedding. Her servant, Bina, a young girl of Gullah ancestry, heard the omen of her mistress' death with the appearance of an owl tapping on the side of the house. Bayard died one week to the day after his young bride-to-be, of the same dreaded fever. The couple is buried in the Bayard family mausoleum on the island. Listen for the haunting hooves the next time a tempest strikes!

Ghosts

DO YOU BELIEVE IN GHOSTS?

Sports Stuff

- **Althea Gibson**—tennis player named Outstanding Woman Athlete in 1957 by the Associated Press; South Carolina Hall of Fame member

- **Larry Doby**—first black baseball player in the American League; first black manager in the American League

- **Alex English**—scoring champion in 1983 for the National Basketball Association (NBA)

- **William "The Refrigerator" Perry**—player for the Chicago Bears Super Bowl team in 1986

Sports Stuff

- **Shoeless Joe Jackson**—baseball player who was said to hit such hard line drives that they would tear the gloves off infielders

- **James Edward Rice**—professional baseball player; led the Boston Red Sox to pennants in 1975 and 1986

- **Joe Frazier**—prize fighter

Entertainers

Eartha Kitt—singer and actress

Andie McDowell—actress

John "Dizzy" Gillespie—jazz trumpeter

Vanna White—TV hostess for *Wheel of Fortune*; letter-turner

Clara Louise Kellogg—turn-of-the-century singer

James Brown—singer; "Godfather of Soul"

Chubby Checker—born Ernest Evans; "King of the Twist"

Entertainers

Whispering Bill Anderson—Columbia, songwriter

Brook Benton, Camden—singer

Robby Benson, Columbia—actor

Hootie and the Blowfish, Columbia—musicians

59

Authors

- **Josephine Humphreys**—contemporary novelist; wrote *Fireman's Fair* and *Dreams of Sleep*
- **Mickey Spillane**—author of detective novels
- **Pat Conroy**—author of *The Lords of Discipline, Beach Music,* and *The Great Santini*
- **Edwin DuBose Heyward**—author and poet; wrote novel *Porgy*; adapted into noted opera *Porgy and Bess*
- **James Dickey**—poet and author
- **Ben Robertson**—20th century author; wrote about cotton farmers in his book *Red Hills and Cotton*
- **Gwen Bristow**—playwright, reporter for *The Times Picayune*; best-known for her historical fiction *The Plantation Trilogy, This Side of Glory,* and *Celia Garth*
- **Elizabeth Boatwright Coker**—20th century author of historical fiction; wrote *Daughter of Strangers*; South Carolina's First Lady of Letters
- **Henry Timrod**—poet laureate of the Confederacy, taught and wrote throughout the state
- **Julia Peterkin**—novelist; Pulitzer prize winner for *Scarlet Sister Mary*
- **Peggy Parrish**—author of the *Amelia Bedelia* series of books for children

Artists

Charles Fraser—painted more than 300 miniatures and 139 paintings in the 18th–19th century

Jasper Johns—noted modern painter; leader in the pop art movement

Henrietta Deering Johnston—17th-century pastel artist; sketched portraits of notable people of the day; her portrait of Colonel William Rhett hangs in Charleston's Gibbes Art Gallery

Alice Ravenel Huger Smith—watercolorist, landscape artist, illustrator, and printmaker of the 20th century

Anna Hyatt Huntington—sculptor of animals; designed Brookgreen Gardens' butterfly-shaped garden and opened the grounds as a showplace for the work of American sculptors

Elizabeth O'Neill Verner—artist specializing in etchings and pastel sketches of Charleston life and culture

Elizabeth White—20th century artist; specialized in oils, etchings, and pencil sketches

Very Important People

Robert Mills—considered to be the most influential architect in early United States history; friend of Thomas Jefferson; designed the Washington Monument and the nation's treasury, post office, and patent office

John Drayton—owner of Drayton Hall; saved his plantation home from destruction by Union troops in 1865 by claiming he was housing smallpox victims

Joel Robert Poinsett—gardener and politician; ambassador to Mexico; returned from Mexico with the plants we now recognize as poinsettias

Very Important People

Broadus Littlejohn—established Community Cash Stores, a chain of markets which offered credit to cash-starved farmers; stores were purchased in 1999 by Acme Markets

Francis Beidler—professional lumberman who called for the preservation of a 6,000 acre (2,400 hectare) blackwater forest of bald cypress and tupelo gum trees, the largest such tract in the world

Ronald McNair—astronaut; second African-American to fly in space; died in the 1986 *Challenger* explosion

More Very Important People

Sara and Angelina Grimke—abolitionists who eventually moved north to Philadelphia, Pennsylvania, where they worked against slavery and for women's rights

Bernard Mannes Baruch—financier, philanthropist, and advisor to presidents; wildlife refuge and institute named after him in Georgetown

Cardinal Joseph Louis Bernardin—Catholic cardinal; awarded Einstein Peace Prize for his work on nuclear disarmament

Thomas Green Clemson—19th century engineer and educator; promoted agricultural colleges; Clemson University named in his honor

David Coker—agriculturalist; developed cotton hybrids

Lane Kirkland—labor leader; president of the American Federation of Labor and Congress of Industrial Organizations (AFL-CIO)

William Stone Hall—20th century doctor who studied mental illness; directed the South Carolina Department of Health

More Very Important People

63

Political Leaders

Wade Hampton—noted Confederate general; governor of South Carolina 1876–79; U.S. Senator 1879–91

Thomas Heyward—signer of the Declaration of Independence; member of the Continental Congress 1776–78

Ernest "Fritz" Hollings—South Carolina governor (1959–63); senator since 1966; chairman of the Senate Commerce Committee

Andrew Jackson—seventh U.S. president; military hero of the 1815 Battle of New Orleans

Henry Laurens—member and president of the Continental Congress (1777–79); negotiated the peace treaty that ended the Revolution

Arthur Middleton—Continental Congress member; signed Declaration of Independence; designed the South Carolina state seal

Charles Pinckney—one of the key architects of the U.S. Constitution; three-time governor of South Carolina; member of the Continental Congress (1784–87)

James "Strom" Thurmond—longest-serving U.S. Senator in history, serving since 1955; governor of South Carolina (1947–51); States' Rights Democrat; presidential candidate (1948)

John C. Calhoun—U.S. Vice President and defender of states' rights; author of resolution called the South Carolina Exposition; considered most famous South Carolina-born politician of the 19th century

Good Guys and Patriots

Mendel Rivers—head of the House Armed Services Committee; encouraged military contractors to open manufacturing plants in Charleston

Pierce Butler—came to South Carolina in the 1760s from Ireland; leader in the Revolution; signer of the U.S. Constitution; first U.S. Senator from South Carolina

Christopher Gadsden—Revolutionary War patriot; nicknamed the "Flame of Liberty"

Francis Marion—known as the "Swamp Fox" during the Revolution for his guerilla tactics against the British forces

Andrew Pickens—Revolutionary War commander; decisive leader in the Battle of Cowpens

Thomas Sumter— nicknamed the Gamecock during the Revolution: used guerilla tactics against British forces; U.S. Senator (1801–1810)

Churches and Schools

CHURCHES
Keeping the Faith

French Huguenot Church, Charleston—located on Church Street, this structure is a fine example of gothic revival architecture

Congregation Beth Elohim, Charleston—birthplace of American Reform Judaism; finest example of Greek revival architecture in the country

First Baptist Church, Columbia—site of the 1860 South Carolina secession convention; escaped destruction during the Civil War when a church sexton directed Federal soldiers to another location

Unitarian Church, Charleston—oldest Unitarian Church in the South; vaulted ceiling based on that of Gloucester Church

Emmanuel African Methodist Episcopal Church, Charleston—home of south's oldest AME congregation

McBee Methodist Church Chapel, Conestee—one of the few octagonal churches remaining in America

SCHOOLS

University of South Carolina, Columbia
Clemson University, Clemson
College of Charleston, Charleston
South Carolina State College, Orangeburg
Medical University of South Carolina, Charleston
Bob Jones University, Greenville
Furman University, Greenville
Baptist College of Charleston
Coker College, Hartsville
Morris College, Sumter
The Citadel, Charleston

Historic Sites and Parks

HISTORIC SITES

Charles Towne Landing, Charleston—marks site of the first permanent English settlement in South Carolina; includes gardens, museum, animal forest, and replica of a 17th century sailing vessel

Angel Oak, Johns Island—1,400 year-old historic live oak tree which is named after plantation owners Justus and Martha Angel; tree is more than 25 feet (8 meters) around, with its largest limb measuring 89 feet (27 meters) long!

PARKS

Old Santee Canal State Park, near Lake Moultrie—contains southern end of the 1800 Santee Canal; first dug channel canal in America

Myrtle Beach State Park—contains 100 acres (40 hectares) of forest along the ocean

Huntington Beach State Park, Murrells Inlet—2,500 acres (1,011 hectares) of salt marsh, tidal creeks, beach, and ruins of *Atalaya*, the studio of sculptor Anna Hyatt Huntington

Hampton Plantation, McLellanville—state park and 18th century home visited by George Washington; also home to Archibald Rutledge, poet laureate of South Carolina

Historic Sites and Parks

67

Home, Sweet Home!

Early Residency

Kershaw-Cornwallis House, Camden—home of Joseph Kershaw, Camden's founder; destroyed during Union occupation in 1865, reconstructed based on original design

Elam Sharpe House, Pendleton—typical upcountry townhouse; two-story house with center hallway and one room on each side, on each level

Governor's Mansion, Columbia—1855 two-story stucco structure; original officer's quarters of the state arsenal's military academy

Milford Plantation, Sumter—finest Greek revival residence in the state; has six Corinthian columns, constructed from 1839–41

Jennings-Brown House, Bennettsville—saltbox-style house furnished in 1850s style; used by Union General Frank Blair in 1865 as his headquarters

Home, Sweet Home!

Moreland House, Charleston—built in 1827, this house features a floating foundation of palmetto logs sunk in marshy ground to withstand tremors from earthquakes

Pink House, Charleston—built in early 18th century of Bermuda stone; served as a tavern

Thomas Bee House, Charleston—example of the typical "single house" common to Charleston; single-room wide, with a door facing the side opening onto a garden

Battlefields and Forts

A few of South Carolina's famous Battlefields

- **Ninety Six Historical Site**—location of the first Revolutionary War Battle fought on southern soil
- **Revolutionary War Park**, Camden—92-acre spread, site of the early town of Camden; restored British fortifications and 18th–19th-century houses
- **Cowpens National Battlefield**, Cowpens—site of American victory during the Revolution; park encompasses 845 acres (341 hectares) with trails and restored cabin
- **Kings Mountain National Military Park**, York— covers about 4,000 acres (1,618 hectares); site of one of the fiercest battles of the Revolution, marking a victory for the Patriots

A few of South Carolina's famous Forts

- **Fort Mitchell**, Hilton Head—earthworks fortification overlooking Skull Creek
- **Fort Sumter National Monument**, Charleston—a federal fort situated in Charleston Harbor; first shots of the Civil War fired upon this Union stronghold on April 12, 1861
- **Fort Johnson**, Charleston—Confederate fort on James Island where soldiers fired guns aimed at Fort Sumter
- **Fort Moultrie**, Sullivans Island—site of original palmetto log fort started in 1776; site of Revolutionary war battle; updated fort in use until 1947

Battlefields and Forts

Libraries

Check out the following special South Carolina libraries! (Do you have a library card? Have you worn it out yet?!)

- First library in the American colonies opened in Charleston, 1698

- **South Caroliniana Library** on the campus of the University of South Carolina, built 1840, first separate university library in the nation

- 40 county and regional libraries

- State and university libraries

- Bookmobiles

Libraries

Nancy Jane Day was named South Carolina's first state librarian over black and white schools in 1946.

70

Zoos and Attractions

- **Charleston Aquarium**
- **Riverbanks Zoo and Botanical Garden**, Columbia
- **Patriot's Point**, Charleston
- **Brookgreen Gardens**, Murrells Inlet
- **White Point Gardens in Battery Park**, Charleston
- **Middleton Place and Gardens**, Charleston
- **Audubon Swamp Garden**, Charleston
- **Santee Coastal Reserve**, Santee
- **Francis Marion National Park**, North Charleston
- **Pinckney Island National Wildlife Refuge**, near Hilton Head Island
- **Cape Romain National Wildlife Refuge**, north of Charleston
- **Gibbes Planetarium**, Columbia
- **South of the Border**, Dillon

Zoos and Attractions

Museums

- **Thoroughbred Hall of Fame**, Aiken
- **Abbeville Opera House**
- **Edisto Island Serpentarium**
- **Florence Air and Missile Museum**
- **Stock Car Hall of Fame/Joe Weatherly Museum**, Darlington
- **The Rice Museum**, Georgetown
- **South Carolina Hall of Fame**, Myrtle Beach
- **Avery Research Center for African-American History and Culture**, Charleston
- **Charleston Museum**
- **Gibbes Museum of Art**, Charleston
- **South Carolina Confederate Relic Room and Museum**, Columbia
- **Greenville County Museum of Art**
- **Discovery Center Museum of Hilton Head Island**
- **South Carolina Railroad Museum**, Winnsboro

Museums

The Confederate submarine *H.L. Hunley*, recently recovered from its sandy grave off Sullivans Island, is now being excavated by archaeologists. Human remains and artifacts are being carefully removed from the ship that went down in 1864.

Monuments and Memorials

Lest We Forget

MONUMENTS

Fort Moultrie National Monument, Sullivans Island—recognizes American Colonel William Moultrie and his men who drove off a squadron of British warships in 1776 during the American Revolution

Fort Sumter National Monument, Charleston—site of the first shots fired in the Civil War

Congaree Swamp National Monument, near Columbia—site of the last significant stand of southern bottomland hardwood forest in the nation

MEMORIALS

Confederate Memorial, Cheraw—oldest Confederate monument in the United States; erected 1867

The Arts

Dock Street Theater, Charleston—first building in the nation designed solely for theatrical performances in 1736

Studio-Museum of Elizabeth O'Neill Verner, Charleston—located in the oldest surviving house in the city; showcases Verner's work

Abbeville Opera House, Abbeville—fully-restored Victorian opera house; featured famous entertainers including Groucho Marx and Fanny Brice

Bi-Lo Center, Greenville—sports and entertainment complex; home to the Greenville Grrrowls East Coast Hockey League Team

Peace Center for the Performing Arts, Greenville—venue featuring Broadway, opera, pop, and classical music performances

South Carolina has 14 symphony orchestras, 35 dance companies, and one major opera company

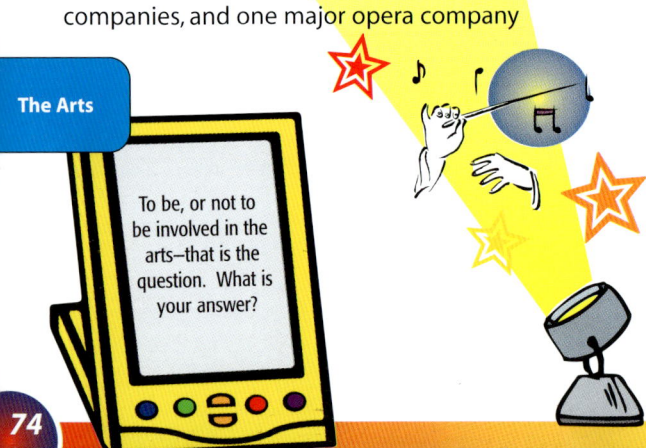

The Arts

> To be, or not to be involved in the arts—that is the question. What is your answer?

Seashores & Lighthouses

SEASHORES

South Carolina's lakes and seashores draw fishermen and tourists from around the world!

Beaches include:
- Myrtle Beach
- Murrells Inlet
- Litchfield Beach
- Folly Beach
- Isle of Palms
- Sullivans Island
- Fripp Island
- Hilton Head Island

LET THERE BE LIGHT!

Lighthouses include:

- Georgetown Lighthouse—oldest active lighthouse in South Carolina
- Cape Romain Lighthouses—twin towers on Cape Romain National Wildlife Refuge
- Morris Island Lighthouse, Charleston—built in 1876
- Sullivan's Island Lighthouse—erected in 1962, part of Coast Guard compound
- Hunting Island Lighthouse—cast iron tower built in 1875
- Hilton Head Lighthouse—built in 1880, one of a few skeletal towers still in existence in the United States
- Harbour Town Lighthouse, Hilton Head Island—functioning tourist attraction; 90-foot (27-meter) lighthouse completed in 1970
- Haig Point, Daufuskie Island—named after plantation owner George Haig

Seashores & Lighthouses

Roads, Bridges, and More!

Roads,

Hwy. 17, coastal route runs from Little River to Bluffton
Cherokee Foothills Scenic Highway, runs from Gaffney to Lake Hartwell on S.C. 11

Bridges,

Cooper River Bridge, Charleston
Ashley River Bridges, Charleston
Savannah River Bridge, connects Georgia and South Carolina

Roads, Bridges, and More!

and More!

Atlantic Intracoastal Waterway, important inland shipping route

Salt Marshes

The lowcountry of South Carolina has large areas of salt marsh which are fertile swampy areas fed simultaneously by saltwater from the sea and freshwater from rivers or streams. They provide a rich feeding ground for shore birds and marine life including crabs, shrimp, fish, and tiny organisms. Some of the largest and most beautiful salt marshes lie between Myrtle Beach and Beaufort.

Huntington Beach State Park, Murrells Inlet—2,500 acres (1,011 hectares) of salt marsh and tidal creeks

Hobcaw Barony—former estate of financier Bernard Baruch near Georgetown; includes North Inlet, 9,000 acres (3,642 hectares) of salt marsh and estuarine area; established as a preserve and natural lab for scientists

Hunting Island State Park, near Beaufort—marshes and forest trails; once a hunting ground for Indians and settlers

Pinckney Island National Wildlife Refuge, near Hilton Head—more than 4,000 acres (1,618 hectares) of salt marsh and small islands

Animals

SOUTH CAROLINA'S ANIMALS INCLUDE:

Snake
Frog
Fox

Squirrel
Shrew
Opossum
Salamander

White-tailed Deer
Black Bear
Raccoon
Cottontail Rabbit
Bobcat
Alligator

Animals

Watch out for picnicking alligators! Murrells Inlet's 'gators love bologna and white bread!

Wildlife Watch

Take a Walk on the Wild Side!

Some endangered South Carolina animals are:

Indiana Bat

West Indian Manatee

Eastern Puma

Leatherback Sea Turtle

Wood Stork

Shortnose Sturgeon

Whales
(finback, humpback, and right)

Red-Cockaded Woodpecker

There are also 13 plants on South Carolina's endangered species list including the Pitcher Plant and Trillium.

Wildlife Watch

Birds

You may spy these birds in South Carolina:

Quail
Duck
Heron
Wild Turkey
Black Skimmer
Tern
Pelican
Rail
Egret
Dove
Wren
Sparrow
Oriole

Birds

A hummingbird's wings beat 75 times a second—so fast that you only see a blur! They make short squeaky sounds but do not sing.

Insects

Don't let these South Carolina bugs bug you!

- Mayfly
- Katydid
- Cricket
- Stick Insect
- Giant Water Bug
- Cicada
- Cockroach
- Ant Lion
- Ladybird Beetle
- Weevil

Dragonfly

Beetle

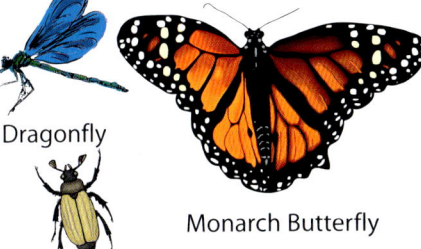

Monarch Butterfly

Tiger Swallowtail

Praying Mantis

Grasshopper

Whirligig beetles have two pairs of eyes—one pair looks above the water, the other under it!

Insects

Do we know any of these bugs?

Maybe... Hey, that ladybug is cute!

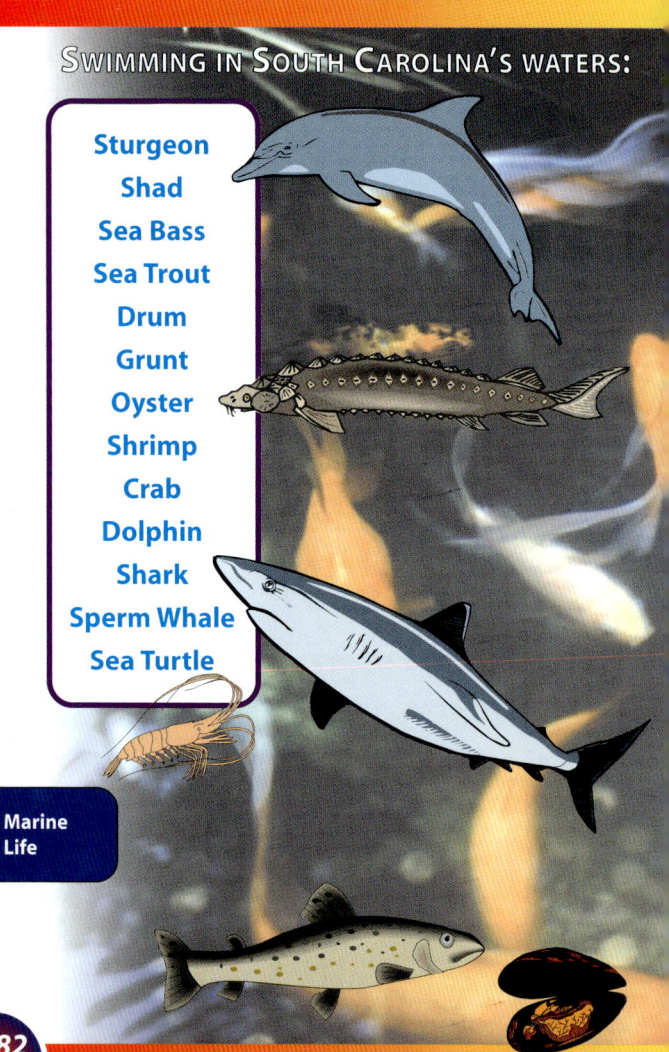

Marine Life

SWIMMING IN SOUTH CAROLINA'S WATERS:

- Sturgeon
- Shad
- Sea Bass
- Sea Trout
- Drum
- Grunt
- Oyster
- Shrimp
- Crab
- Dolphin
- Shark
- Sperm Whale
- Sea Turtle

Marine Life

Pond Critters

In South Carolina's ponds, you may find:

- Bullfrog
- Diving Beetle
- Painted Turtle
- Water Snake
- Eastern Newt
- Catfish
- Freshwater Eel
- Minnow
- Sunfish
- Muskrat

Bait your hook with a little minnow to cast your line into a South Carolina pond for a tasty catfish!

Pond Critters

83

Seashells

She sells seashells by the South Carolina seashore!

Periwinkle

Slipper Shell

Moon Shell

Helmet Shell

Wentletrap

Whelk

Auger Shell

Mussel

Scallop

Cockle

Coquina

Angel Wing

Shipworm

Seashells

If you look carefully, you might catch a glimpse of a ghost crab scurrying into its sandy burrow on the beach!

Trees

TREEMENDOUS!

These trees tower over South Carolina:

- OAK
- LAUREL
- HICKORY
- MAGNOLIA
- GUM
- PINE
- BEECH
- CYPRESS
- HEMLOCK
- MAPLE
- TULIP
- REDBUD

Trees

Wildflowers

Are you crazy about these South Carolina wildflowers and plants?

- Palmetto
- Yucca
- Honeysuckle
- Spanish Moss
- Sweet Bay
- Venus Flytrap
- Azalea
- Mountain Laurel
- Pyxie
- Smilax
- Jessamine
- Dogwood

Wildflowers

Flower Power!

Cream of the Crops

Agricultural products from South Carolina:

- Tobacco
- Soybeans 
- Corn 
- Peach 
- Cotton 
- Apples 
- Hay 
- Oats 
- Peanuts 
- Tomatoes 
- Watermelons 
- Eggs 
- Cattle 
- Hogs 
- Turkeys 
- Tea

Cream of the Crops

87

Firsts and Onlys

● South Carolina was the **first state to secede** from the Union prior to the Civil War.

● Colonel William Moultrie was the first American **to defeat the British** during the Revolution at present-day Fort Moultrie, then called Fort Sullivan on Sullivan's Island.

● The **first shots of the Civil War** were fired on Fort Sumter by Confederate soldiers stationed in Charleston.

● The Charleston Tea Company is the **only working tea plantation** in the United States.

● The world's **first department store** is located in Charleston.

Firsts and Onlys

Festivals

celebrate!

Spoleto Festival USA, Charleston—counterpart of the Spoleto Festival in Italy; series of music, dance, and theater; performances held in May

Gullah Festival, Beaufort—showcases the fine arts, customs, and language of the black sea island culture called Gullah

South Carolina Peach Festival, Gaffney—10 days of concerts, sporting events, peaches, and a parade; held in June

Southeastern Wildlife Exposition, Charleston—paintings, sculptures, photographs, and more relating to fish, birds, and mammals; held in February

Mayfest, Columbia—largest arts and entertainment festival in the state's capital

Carolina Cup, Camden—thoroughbred steeplechases and flat racing; held in April

Watermelon Festival, Pageland—clogging, art and watermelon seed spittin'; held in July

Chitlin' Strut, Salley—enjoy deep-fried pig intestines at this long-running November festival

Holidays

Calendar

General Robert E. Lee's Birthday, *January 9*	Martin Luther King, Jr. Day, *3rd Monday in January*	Groundhog Day, *February 2*
Presidents' Day, *3rd Monday in February*	Memorial Day, *last Monday in May*	Independence Day, *July 4*
Labor Day, *1st Monday in September*	Columbus Day, *2nd Monday in October*	Veterans Day, *November 11*
		Thanksgiving, *4th Thursday in November*

South Carolina celebrates its admission to the U.S. on May 23, 1788.

Holidays

Christmas, Chanukah, Kwanza, Vietnamese Tet, and Chinese New Year are all special celebrations in South Carolina

Famous Food

South Carolina is famous for...

the following foods!

Hot Buttered Grits
Roasted Oysters
She-Crab Soup
Pork Barbecue
Low Country Boil
Barbecued Ribs
Cornbread

Collard Greens
Chicken Bog
Rice
Ham Biscuits
Fried Shrimp
Benne Seed Wafers
Sugary Pralines

Yum, yum. This is great!

Let's dig in!

Famous Food

Business & Trade

South Carolina Works!

South Carolina has a diverse economy with several major industries including textiles, paper, and paper products. Chemical production, machinery, and automobile manufacturing also contribute to the state's economy. Manufacturing provides about 500,000 jobs statewide.

Agriculture has dropped in importance, although tobacco, soybeans, cotton, and corn are still planted. Tourism, particularly along the Grand Strand and in Charleston, adds to the state's economy.

Ships from around the world sail into South Carolina's major port city of Charleston. The state's two other ports are in Georgetown and Port Royal.

Business & Trade

State Books & Websites

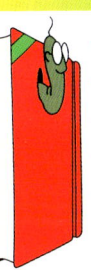

My First Book About South Carolina by Carole Marsh
America the Beautiful: South Carolina by Deborah Kent
Kids Learn America by Patricia Gordon and Reed C. Snow
From Sea to Shining Sea: South Carolina by Dennis B. Fradin
Let's Discover the States: South Carolina by the Aylesworths
The South Carolina Experience Series by Carole Marsh

Cool South Carolina Websites

http://www.state.sc.us

http://www.southcarolinaexperience.com

http://www.50states.com

http://www.netstate.com

Glossary

South Carolina Glossary

Glossary Words

coast—land along the sea
civil rights—the rights of a citizen
gamecock—a fighting rooster
grits—ground hominy
hurricanes—a very strong windstorm; often with heavy rain
immigrant—a person who comes to a new country
mansion—a large, stately house
mausoleum—a large tomb
nullify—cancel; make useless
patriots—people who love and support their country
planter—owner of a plantation
revolution—the overthrow of a government
salt marsh—marshy, boggy area fed by salt and fresh water
secede—to stop being a member of some group
shag—a dance common to coastal South Carolina
tourists—people who visit a place

Spelling List

South Carolina Spelling Bee

Here are some special South Carolina-related words to learn! To take the Spelling Bee, have someone call out the words and you spell them aloud or write them on a piece of paper.

Spelling Words

- architect
- agriculture
- climate
- colonists
- Confederate
- diplomat
- environment
- festival
- ghost
- governor
- lighthouse
- museum
- nickname
- oysters
- resort
- sea island
- seaport
- slave
- theater
- tourism

About the Author

ABOUT THE AUTHOR...

CAROLE MARSH has been writing about South Carolina for more than 20 years. She is the author of the popular *South Carolina State Stuff Series* for young readers and creator along with her son, Michael Marsh, of *South Carolina Facts and Factivities*, a CD-ROM widely used in South Carolina schools. The author of more than 100 South Carolina books and other supplementary educational materials on the state, Marsh is currently working on a new collection of South Carolina materials for young people. Marsh correlates her South Carolina materials to the South Carolina learning standards. Many of her books and other materials have been inspired by or requested by South Carolina teachers and librarians.

You know... that was a great experience!

Sure was! Thanks for taking me along.

EDITORIAL ASSISTANTS:
Michele Yother • Pat Newman

GRAPHIC DESIGNER:
Al Fortunatti